YOU MUST BE JOKING, TWO!

You Must Be Joking, Two!

Even Cooler Jokes,
Plus 11 1/2 Tips for
Laughing Yourself into
Your Own Stand-Up
Comedy Routine

written and
illustrated by

PAUL BREWER

Cricket Books
Chicago

No part of this publication may be reproduced in whole or in part, or stored
in a retrieval system, or transmitted in any form or by any means, electronic,
mechanical, photocopying, recording, or otherwise, without the written
permission of the publisher. For information regarding permission, write to
Carus Publishing Company, 315 Fifth Street, Peru, Illinois 61354.

Library of Congress Cataloging-in-Publication Data
Brewer, Paul.
  You must be joking, two! : even cooler jokes, plus 11½ tips for laughing
yourself into your own stand-up comedy routine / written and illustrated by
Paul Brewer.— 1st ed.
    p. cm.
  ISBN–13: 978-0-8126-2752-7
  ISBN–10: 0-8126-2752-0
  1. Wit and humor, Juvenile. I. Title. II. Title: You must be joking, 2!

PN6166.B74 2007
818'.5402—dc22

2007014450

For Jacqui and Anatoli Ignatov,
Melanie and Ethan Brewer

Contents

Introduction

Here it is, the long-awaited sequel to *You Must Be Joking!* (Well, at least I think it's the long-awaited sequel.)

As with my first book, *You Must Be Joking, Two!* is loaded with very funny jokes about monsters, aliens, cyberspace, food, school, and a bunch of other topics that should definitely crack you up. The final chapter, "11½ Tips for Laughing Yourself into Your Own Stand-Up Comedy Routine," includes awesome advice on how to become a better joke-teller. I'll also show you how you can take joke-telling to the next level by getting up in front of an audience just like a real stand-up comedian. I'll give you ideas for creating a wacky costume that will make people laugh. Throw in a few silly props such as a horn or a rubber chicken, and people will laugh even harder. Add your own special comedy style, and TA-DA! you'll have them laughing their heads off.

Being funny is really quite simple. You can start by looking for the humor in everyday situations. Say you're watching TV with your friends, and a really bad car commercial comes on. The announcer is practically screaming, "Just $199 down and $199 a month puts you in this fine used car!" Here's your cue to use "observational humor," or humor inspired by everyday life. Come up with a crazy-sounding voice to mimic the announcer. Mess up your hair and gesture wildly while you shout, "Just $1.99 down and $1.99 a month puts you in this really cheap piece of junk!" This should get a few laughs out of your friends.

You can only memorize a certain number of jokes, but once you find the humor in whatever's happening around you, you're set for life. Pay attention, keep up with current events, and write things down that you think are funny. Who knows? You might be able to turn them into jokes later on. Almost everything can be funny, and if you can find humor wherever you go, you'll never run out of material. Humor is like air. It's everywhere.

How often does being funny come in handy? Well, if your brother or sister is picking on you, try saying something crazy like this: "You can pick on me, or you can pick your nose. Could you pleeeese just pick your nose?" That might crack them up enough so they stop being mean to you. Humor also improves your health—it's a fact that laughing releases body chemicals called endorphins that make you feel good. You could be helping the health of everyone around you simply by being funny and making people laugh.

Just as in my first book, the end of each joke chapter has the setup for a riddle, but no punch line. Your job is to come up with one. You'll find an answer printed upside down at the bottom of the page, but your answer may not be the same as mine. It might be funnier! At the end of the "11½ Tips," you'll see an illustration of a famous comedian on a stage telling a joke. As with the other chapters, I'll give you the riddle setup first. See if you can identify the comedian and come up with a punch line for the riddle.

Now, it's on to the jokes. On your marks, get set, laugh!

—*Paul Brewer*
www.paulbrewer.com
www.youmustbejoking.net

Screams of Laughter

Two police officers in New York City are watching King Kong climb to the top of the Empire State Building.

One says to the other, "Why do you think he's in such a hurry?"

"Oh, that's obvious," replies his partner. "He's got a plane to catch."

What do you do if King Kong sits in front of you at the movie theater?
Miss the entire movie!

What's big and hairy, wears makeup and a
   dress, and climbs up the Empire State
   Building?
Queen Kong.

What kind of TV does Dracula own?
A plasma.

What's the tallest building in Transylvania?
The Vampire State Building.

Why did Godzilla wrap a long string around
   a city in Japan?
So he could turn it into a Tokyo-yo.

Who's the clumsiest monster of all?
Clodzilla.

What do you get if you cross a monster with
   a Boy Scout?
A creature that scares old ladies across the
   street.

Why do witches wear nametags?
So they know which witch is which.

Why doesn't the Mummy ever take a vacation?
He's afraid he'll relax and unwind.

What happened to the woman who didn't pay
her exorcist?
She was repossessed.

A man shows up at the hospital complaining
that he has swallowed a monster. He demands
that they perform surgery on him to remove
it, and nothing his doctor says will make him
change his mind.

After discussing the situation with her
staff, the doctor decides to fool the man into
thinking that they removed his imaginary
monster.

The next morning the patient is wheeled
into the operating room and put into a deep
sleep. When the man wakes up, the doctor
is standing next to his bed with a little green
monster on a leash.

"The operation was a total success, and we
removed the monster," says the doctor.

"Who are you trying to kid?" says the man.
"The monster I swallowed was purple!"

What do French skeletons say before they
   begin eating?
Bone appétit!

How do you make a
skeleton laugh?

Answer: Tickle its funny bone.

Jokes from
Outer Space

Jacqui: I was working at the coffee shop this
morning, and I saw some flying saucers.
Melanie: No way. You're kidding, right?
Jacqui: No, I'm not kidding. I tripped on
a floor mat, and a stack of saucers
went flying!

How does the Man in the Moon cut his hair?
E-clipse it!

If the Man in the Moon gets married, will he
and his wife go on a honey-earth?

Which planet is like the circus?
Saturn, because it has three rings.

Why do black holes like eating comets
the most?
Because they're meteor.

What treats do space aliens like to get on
Halloween?
Milky Ways, Moon Pies, and Mars Bars.

What do you get when you cross an alien
  spacecraft with an elephant?
A flying saucer that won't take off.

What phone service do extraterrestrials use?
E T & T.

Why do aliens from outer space like to fly
    to Earth so much?
Because of all the frequent flyer miles
    they get!

If Martians live on Mars and Venusians live
on Venus, what lives on Pluto?
Fleas.

What do you call a crazy insect that lives on
the Moon?
A lunar-tic.

And when does a lunar-tic act the craziest?
When there's a full Earth.

An alien spaceship was running low on fuel,
so it landed at a gas station in the middle of
the desert. On one side of the spacecraft were
printed the letters "UFO."

The station attendant was completely
stunned as he came out to see what was going
on. Pointing to the side of the spacecraft, he
asked, "I'll bet that stands for unidentified
flying object, right?"

"Nope," said one of the aliens. "It stands
for unleaded fuel only."

Why did NASA send Mickey Mouse into
outer space?
To help find Pluto.

**What did the alien say
when he walked into his spaceship?**

Answer: "Ouch!"

Two, Four, Six, Eight, and No-Legged Funnies

What's smarter than a talking bird?
A spelling bee.

If you tell a cow a funny joke, and she starts
  laughing, would milk come squirting out
  her nose?

Mel: Hey, look—it's a baby snake.
Kathy: How do you know it's a baby?
Mel: I can tell by its rattle.

How do you stop a rooster from crowing on
    Sunday morning?
Have him for dinner on Saturday night.

What might you get if you sit behind a cow?
A pat on the head!

A boy with an elephant stuck to his head went
to see a doctor. After a few minutes of waiting,
he was led back to the examining room.

    "Well, well, it sure looks like you have a big
problem," said the doctor.

    "Yes I do," replied the elephant. "Could
you get this kid off my foot!"

Why can't two elephants go swimming?
Because they only have one pair of trunks.

What do you get if you cross insects with a
    rabbit?
Bugs Bunny.

What do you get if you cross a famous whale
    with a cow?
Shamooooooo!

Robert: My pig lost his voice.
Susanne: No kidding. Is he upset?
Robert: Oh yeah, he's disgruntled!

Ethan: If spiders were as big as horses, it wouldn't be so bad.
Christian: Are you kidding? Why would you say that?
Ethan: Because if you get bit by one, you could just ride it to the hospital.

What kind of dog loves bubble baths?
A shampoodle.

What do you get when you cross an ape with
a flower?
A chimp-pansy.

Two sheep are quietly grazing in a field on a
beautiful summer day in Ireland. After a few
moments of munching away, one of the sheep
raises her head and blurts out, "BAAAAAAA!"
The other sheep raises her head, looks
over, and says, "I was just going to say that!"

What's the difference between a dog and a
flea?
A dog can have fleas, but a flea can't have
dogs.

Calvin: My brother just swallowed a frog.
Ralph: Is he O.K.?
Calvin: Well, he might croak any minute.

What's worse than raining cats and dogs?
Hailing taxicabs.

How do you stop an elephant from charging?

Answer: Take away its credit card.

Laptop
Laughs

If Abraham Lincoln had owned a computer, he would have lived in a "blog cabin"!

What's a laptop's least favorite children's book?
Green Eggs and Spam.

Nicholas: Have you ever logged on to www.amnesia.net?
Sarah: Sorry, but I just don't remember.

Customer: I just cleaned my computer, and now it doesn't work at all.

Repairman: What did you clean it with?

Customer: Soap and water.

Repairman: Don't you know you're not supposed to use water to clean a computer?

Customer: Oh, it wasn't the water that caused the problem. It was putting it in the dryer!

What does Harry Potter use to correct his magic?

The spell checker.

Customer: I need a pair of glasses for my computer.

Computer Salesperson: A pair of glasses. Why on earth for?

Customer: To improve its Web site!

Why did the chicken cross the Web?

To get to the other site.

Why did the computer cross the road?

To get a byte to eat.

Computer Technician: Hello. May I help you?

Woman on phone: Yes, my computer is acting very strangely. It's shaking, sweating, making sort of a wheezing sound, and it's very hot to the touch. What do you think the problem is?

Computer Technician: Oh, it's probably just a virus.

What did the little laptop cry?
"I want my data!"

What do computer programmers like to read?
Dot comics.

How did the convict use his computer to break out of prison?

Answer: He hit the escape key.

Jokes with Class

Teacher: What's 22 plus 28?

Pablo: 50.

Teacher: That's good.

Pablo: Good, are you kidding? That's perfect!

Mom: Why are you home from school so early?

Sean: I was the only one who could answer a question.

Mom: Oh, really. What was the question?

Sean: Who threw the eraser at the chalkboard?

Dad: Why are you doing so poorly in history?

Emily: Because the teacher keeps asking me about stuff that happened way before I was born!

Teacher: O.K., class, here's a question. If corn oil comes from corn, olive oil from olives, and peanut oil from peanuts, does anyone know where baby oil comes from?

Ethan: Babies!

Teacher: Jason, this assignment that you've turned in is barely a page long. It's not what I asked you to do. Your instructions were to write a five-page report about milk.

Jason: It's about condensed milk!

Ana: I wish I had been born in prehistoric times.

Teacher: Why is that?

Ana: No history to study!

Teacher: Kevin, can you tell me what a
  thesaurus is?
Kevin: Um, I think it's a dinosaur that
  worked in the library.

Allison: Hey, Mom, I learned how to write today.

Mom: That's great! What did you write?

Allison: I don't know because I haven't learned how to read yet.

Teacher: So tell me, Alex, are you good in science?

Alex: Well, yes and no.

Teacher: What do you mean by that?

Alex: Yes, I'm no good in science.

Teacher: What are the Great Plains?

Anatoli: The 747, the Concorde, and the F-16.

The Spanish explorers sailed around the world in galleons.
How many galleons did they get to the mile?

Who invented King Arthur's round table?

Answer: Sir Cumference!

Jokes So Good You Can Eat Them

Waiter! Waiter! I've counted nineteen flies in this bowl of soup.

One more and you'll beat the *Guinness Book of World Records*!

Waiter! Waiter! This soup tastes funny.

Then why aren't you laughing?

Waiter! Waiter! What's this bug in my soup?

Oh gosh, I don't know, madam. We have so many different kinds here.

Waiter! Waiter! There's a mosquito in my
soup.
Sorry, sir. But we're fresh out of flies today.

Waiter! Waiter! There's a fly in my soup.
What do you expect for a few bucks?
A beetle?

Waitress: How did you find your steak, sir?
Customer: Well, I looked and looked, and
there it was, hiding under a French fry.

Customer: Is there chili on the menu?
Waitress: There was, but I wiped it off.

Élan: What do you think of raisin bread?
Janell: I don't know. I've never raised any.

Why did the apple go out with the plum?
He couldn't find a date.

What did the chef say when he dropped
some waffles on the floor?
"How waffle!"

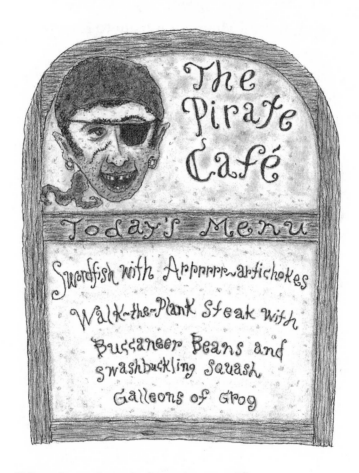

What is a pirate's favorite meal?
Swordfish with arrrrrrr-artichokes.

Janice: Where do omelets come from?
Amir: Eggplants.

What's gray and white on the inside, red and
white on the outside, and comes in a can?
Campbell's Cream of Elephant Soup.

Why did the woman wear a helmet at the
dinner table?
She was on a crash diet.

Why was the ketchup embarrassed?

Answer: It saw the salad dressing.

A Laugh a Day
Keeps the
Doctor Away

Doctor! Doctor! I've swallowed a bone.
Are you choking?
No, I'm not kidding. I really did!

Doctor! Doctor! I get pains in the eye when
   I drink coffee.
Have you tried taking the spoon out of
   the cup?

Patient: Doctor, when my grandfather turned
   sixty-five, he started running.
Doctor: It's good to hear that a man of his
   age wants to stay in shape. So what's
   the problem?
Patient: Well, he's seventy now, and we have
   no idea where he is!

Doctor! Doctor! I keep thinking I'm a goat.
How long have you felt like that?
Ever since I was a kid.

Doctor! Doctor! I think my eyesight is
   getting worse.
It certainly is. This is a jewelry store.

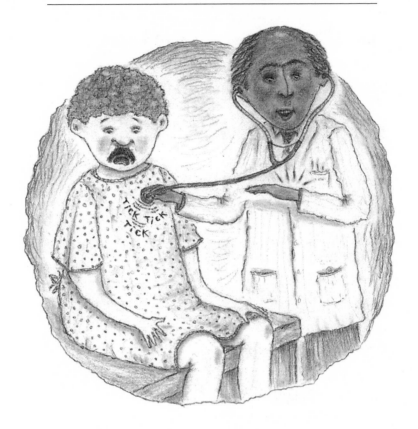

Doctor! Doctor! I've developed a double
    heartbeat since my operation.
Well, that explains where my wrist
    watch went!

Nurse: Doctor Moe, there's an invisible man
    here to see you. He's in the waiting room.
Doctor Moe: Tell him I can't see him.

Doctor! Doctor! When I press with my finger
here, it hurts . . . and here, it hurts . . . and
here, it hurts again. What do you think is
wrong with me?

You have a broken finger.

Doctor! Doctor! How do I cure my
sleepwalking?

Put bubble wrap on your bedroom floor.

Doctor! Doctor! I snore so loud I keep myself
awake. What should I do?

Sleep in another room.

Doctor! Doctor! I keep seeing green and
   purple spots.
Have you seen a psychiatrist?
No, just the green and purple spots.

**Which of the fifty states
is a doctor?**

Answer: MD.

Knock, Knock!

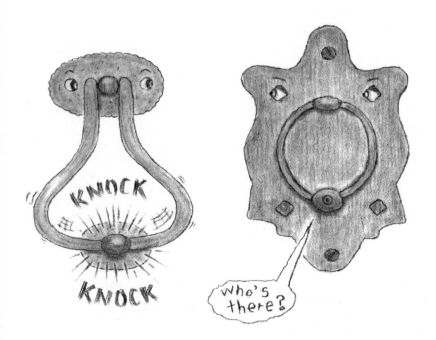

Knock, knock.
Who's there?
Abe Lincoln.
Abe Lincoln who?
Are you kidding, you don't know who
    Abe Lincoln is?

Knock, knock.
Who's there?
Turnip.
Turnip who?
Turnip the music and let's boogie!

Knock, knock.
Who's there?
Gopher.
Gopher who?
Who wants to gopher a pizza?

Knock, knock.
Who's there?
Allied!
Allied who?
Allied, so sue me!

Knock, knock.
Who's there?
Cows.
Cows who?
No, owls hoo. Cows moo.

Knock, knock.
Who's there?
Radio.
Radio who?
Radio not, here I come.

Knock, knock.
Who's there?
Gorilla.
Gorilla who?
Gorilla me a cheeseburger. I'm hungry!

Knock, knock.
Who's there?
Wilma.
Wilma who?
Wilma dinner be ready soon?

Knock, knock.
Who's there?
Rita.
Rita who?
Rita book, you might learn something.

Tim: Dock, dock.
Ed: Dock, dock? I thought it was knock, knock.
Tim: Eh ith. Buh I hab a tewible code.

Knock, knock.
Who's there?
A little girl who can't reach the doorbell!

Knock, knock.
Who's there?
Tank.
Tank who?

Answer: Oh, you're welcome!

Name That Joke or Joke That Name

What do you call a man
with a shovel?

Doug.

What do you call a guy who likes to float in
the water?
Bob.

What do you call a man on the edge of
a mountain?
Cliff.

What name has a nice ring?
Belle.

What do you call a guy you put up on a wall?
Art.

What do you call someone lying on the
    doorstep?
Matt.

What do you call a girl who wakes up early?
Dawn.

What do you call someone who puts gas in
    your car?
Phillip.

What do you call a dude with a dollar?
Buck.

What do you call a boy with a beak?
Bill.

What do you call a guy who rolls in
the leaves?
Russell.

What do you call a man with a lot of money?
Rich.

What do you call a snowman in the spring?
Puddle.

What do you get if you throw meat, carrots, celery, tomatoes, broth, and spices into a pot?
Stu.

What do you call a lady who sings?
Carol.

What do you call a guy who makes wigs?

Answer: Harry.

Fiddle with Riddles

what do you call a . . .
. . . do you get if you cross a . . .
What do you get if . . .
What do you get when you . . .

What kind of movies do pirates like?
*Arrrrrrrr-*rated.

Which pirate was always joking around?
Captain Kidd.

What do you call a dinosaur that smashes
    everything in its path?
Tyrannosaurus wrecks!

What can you catch with peanut butter?
Jellyfish.

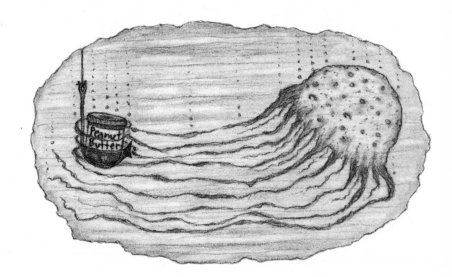

What did the snail say when it rode on the
    turtle's back?
Wheeeeeeeeeeeeeeeeeeeeeeeeeeeeeee!

What did one elevator say to another
    elevator?
"I think I'm coming down with something."

What did one mind reader say to the other
    mind reader when they met?
"You're just fine. How am I?"

What do Christopher Columbus, George
    Washington, and Abraham Lincoln
    have in common?
They were all born on holidays.

What do you get when you cross a jeweler
    with a plumber?
A ring around the bathtub.

What do you get if you cross a cheetah
    with a hamburger?
Fast food.

What do you get if you cross a dinosaur
with a pig?
Jurassic Pork.

What do you get when you cross Bambi
with a ghost?
Bam-boo!

What happened when the werewolf
  swallowed a clock?
He got ticks.

What do people do in clock factories?
They make faces all day.

What has fifty right legs and can't walk?
Half a centipede.

What's the best time to go to the dentist?
When it's tooth-hurty!

**What do you get if you cross
a bear with a skunk?**

Answer: Winnie-the-Phew.

Game
of Giggles

What do basketball players and babies
have in common?
They both dribble all over the place!

What's the difference between a football
player and his tired dog?
The ballplayer wears a complete uniform,
but the dog only pants!

Why did the wrestler bring a key into the ring?
To get him out of any headlocks.

Jennifer: Guess what, Mom? I'm trying out
for the cross-country ski team.
Mom: Oh dear, that sounds hard. Could you
at least start with a small country?

Teacher: Can someone name the four seasons?
Max: Football, basketball, baseball, and
soccer.

What do donuts and basketballs have
in common?
People like to dunk both of them.

TV Reporter: What's the hardest thing you do every day?

Basketball Star: Bend down to tie my shoes.

Cyrus: Why are those three football players different heights?

Gary: I think the tall one's a fullback, the middle one's a halfback, and the small one's a quarterback.

Carleton: What's the score?

Ken: Fourteen to seven.

Carleton: Who's winning?

Ken: Fourteen.

Why did the woman go running every time she forgot something important?

She was trying to jog her memory.

Why does it take longer to run from second base to third base than it does from first to second?

Because there's a short stop between second and third.

Why shouldn't you tell jokes while ice-skating?

Because the ice might crack up.

What do you get when you tie two bikes
together?
Siamese Schwinns!

Why did the boy build a mountain bike
out of trash?
He wanted to re-cycle.

What kind of motorcycle does a
comedian ride?
A Yamaha-ha-ha!

Why does a bike stand on one leg?
Because it's two-tired.

Why did the cops show up at the baseball game?

Answer: Someone stole the bases!

Why Did the . . . ?

Why did the dinosaur cross the road?
Because chickens weren't around yet.

Why didn't the chicken cross the road?
Because she was chicken!

Why did the rooster cross the road?
To prove he wasn't a chicken.

Why did the duck cross the road?
It was the chicken's day off.

Why did the poodle cross the road?
To get to the barking lot.

Why did the children cross the playground?
To get to the other slide.

Why did the people cross the road?
Because there was a fried chicken stand
    on the other side.

Why didn't the skeleton cross the road?
He had no body to go with him.

Why did the car stop running when it
   saw a ghost?
It had a nervous breakdown.

Why did the clown go to the doctor?
Because she was feeling funny.

Why did the dweeb put a clock under
   his desk?
He was told to work over-time.

Why did the octopus use so much
    deodorant?
You would too if you had that many arms!

Why did the chicken cross the road?
Don't ask me, ask the chicken!

**Why did the chicken stop
crossing the road?**

**Answer: Because it was tired of people
making all those jokes about her.**

Big Dilemmas

What do you get if you cross a freeway with
    a chicken?
Run over!

A man was caught for speeding and had to go
before a judge.

"I have the option of giving you three days
in jail, or $300," said the judge.

The man quickly replied, "I'll take the
money, Your Honor!"

Ms. Krull's second-grade class was on a field
trip to their local police station.

A student, Lisa, saw several pictures
tacked to a bulletin board. Lisa pointed to a
picture and asked, "Is that really a photo
of one of the ten most wanted criminals
in the world?"

"Yes," said the police officer. "And we want
very badly to capture him."

Lisa thought about it for a few seconds,
then replied, "Well, why didn't you just keep
him when you took his picture?"

A man is driving along in his car when his wife calls him on his cell phone.

"Honey, be careful. I just heard on the news that there's a car on the freeway driving the wrong way."

The man replies, "Only one, are you kidding? There must be hundreds of them!"

Frédérique: My stupid dog has to go to
   court!
Kathy: Oh really. Why's that?
Frédérique: He got a barking ticket!

Police Officer: I'm sorry, ma'am, but I have
   to ticket you for driving 100 miles an hour.
Woman: But that's impossible, Officer. I've
   only been driving for fifteen minutes.

Why don't they serve chocolate in prison?
Because it makes you break out!

Two boys arrive late to class one morning and are immediately confronted by their teacher.

"O.K., what's your excuse this time?" says the teacher to the first boy.

"I was in a deep sleep, dreaming I was doing my homework. I was working so hard that I didn't want to wake up and lose everything I'd completed."

"So what's your excuse?" says the teacher to the other boy.

"I was helping him!"

Two kids were camping out in their backyard one night. They wanted to know what time it was. To find out, they began singing a very silly song as loud as they possibly could.

Eventually one of the neighbors threw open her window and shouted, "What do you think you're doing out there? Don't you know it's three o'clock in the morning!"

What kind of clothes do lawyers wear?

Answer: Law-suits.

Hugh Maika Melaff

Super Silly Songs

Baby, I Need Some Smoochin' by Wanda
    Kissmee
Piggin' Out by I. Aida Lott
Won Me Over by Wade Tu Goh
Air Guitar Boogie by Rock N. Role

Perfect Love by U. R. Thuhwon
See You Later by Mae B. Tomorrow
You Cheated and Lied by Y. R. Eusobadd
I Totally Rule! by Hugo Gurll

A Song for You by A. Mel O'Dee

Are You Gonna Leave Me? by Ima Dianne
　　Toonoe

Must-See Movies

The Wacky Poodle, starring Kir Lee Mutt and
　　Fran Chi Dawggy

The Evil Snake, starring Sir Pent and Bo
 Aakuhn Striktor
Genie in a Bottle, starring Buff N. Delantern
 and Will Granta Wish
I Was a Teenage Nose-Picker, starring Les
 Pikkem and Will Flickem
The Killer Vampires, starring Pearce Nex and
 E. Drew Blood
The Coldest Place on Earth, starring Ann
 Tarctic and I. M. Freesing
Lost Love, starring U. R. Gonn and I. B. Blue
Out of Control, starring Randy Redd Lyte and
 Krash D. Carr
Alien Invaders, starring Mart Shunn and
 X. Trey Terrestrial
Journey to the Sun, starring Les Turner Round
 and I. M. Berninghupp

Offbeat Books

The End Is Near by U. B. Warned
Dental Dilemma by O. Penn Jaw
The Mystery of the Lost Report Card by Lou
 Sing Stoff

The Beach Barbecue Disaster by Minnie Sandy Berger

Teaching Babies to Draw by Mark N. DeWall

A Doctor's Guide to Tetanus Shots by Dr. Juan Rusty Nale

My Life of Crime by Robb N. Banks

I Never Drive by Wendy Rhodes Wett

Herbs to the Rescue by Justin Thyme

A Painful Situation by Lance A. Boyle

If the author of a joke book is R. U. Krakenupp, what's the title?

Answer: *You Must Be Joking, Two!*

Easy as Pie

What would you call a joke book for chickens?
A yolk book.

What kind of elephants live in Antarctica?
Very cold ones.

What is H_2O_4?
Taking a bath!

What do prisoners use to call each other?
Cell phones.

What do you call a fly with no wings?
A walk.

What do you call a fish with two knees?
A tu-knee fish!

When is a car like a frog?
When it's being toad.

Where do fish go to borrow money?
The loan shark.

What do you call a bull who can tell jokes?
Laugh-a-bull.

Where would you get the freshest milk shake?
From a cow during an earthquake.

What building has the most stories?
The library.

What does a snowman have for breakfast?
Snow-flakes.

What is the quickest way to double
    your money?
Fold it in half.

What is the opposite of cock-a-doodle-doo?
Cock-a-doodle-don't.

What do you use to fix a broken tomato?
Tomato paste.

How do you make a hot dog stand?
Take away its chair.

What kind of key opens a banana?

Answer: A monkey.

11 1/2 Tips for Laughing Yourself into Your Own Stand-Up Comedy Routine

In my last book, I told you how to remember, tell, and make up your own jokes. Now I'll show you how you can put together your own stand-up comedy routine.

The Tips

1. First, you need jokes, and this book is a good start. You can find other joke books at bookstores and libraries. A *huge* source for jokes is the Internet. Just Google "kids' jokes" and you'll find zillions of them. And, of course, if you hear a good joke somewhere, memorize it or write it down so you don't forget it.

2. Riddles are fun to tell and fairly easy to make up. A list of homonyms (words that sound alike but have different meanings) is great for making up riddles. Here's a good example using *carat* (a diamond measurement) and *carrot* (a vegetable that rabbits like):

What do you give a rabbit on her
wedding day?
A three-*carrot* ring.

Here's another that uses *bear* (an animal)
to mean *bear* (put up with):

Why don't grizzlies like to live
in the desert?
They can't *bear* the heat.

Knock-knocks are even easier to make up. The trick is to use words that rhyme or have double meanings. A good place to start is with a rhyming dictionary. A book of baby names or a list of names off the Internet will also help. Just read and get creative.

> Knock, knock.
> *Who's there?*
> Doris.
> *Doris who?*
> Doris open. Come on in!

3. Watch other comedians to see how they make people laugh. Don't forget about old black-and-white movies and TV shows starring classic comedians from the past. Silent movie star Charlie Chaplin wore a funny mustache and dressed up in a baggy suit with a bowler hat, a cane, and shoes too big for his feet. Groucho Marx was famous for his curly hair, grease paint eyebrows and mustache, wire-rimmed glasses, and a fat cigar. Red-haired comedian Lucille Ball wore all kinds of crazy costumes on her TV show; she even dressed up as Charlie Chaplin and Groucho Marx's brother Harpo. These comedians' appearance and behavior were much more exaggerated than those of comedians today. Just looking at them made you laugh. They didn't necessarily tell jokes; they were funny because of all the crazy things they said and did. Wearing funny costumes and makeup was part of their act, and it made their comedy a much more visual experience. They were brilliant.

4. After you've watched other comedians, you'll want to create your own comedic character—who you become when you tell your jokes. Maybe you'll want to play it straight and be yourself, and that can work just fine. But you also might want to put together a costume from a hat, an oversized coat, colorful scarfs, lots of jewelry, or whatever's around the house. Add a funny hair style and a little makeup, and you're on your way. Dressing up like a circus clown and doing your act is something you don't see every day, but it could be hysterical. Try using funny cartoon voices and exaggerated facial expressions and hand gestures to move your comedy along.

How you stand and walk is also an important part of your act. Charlie Chaplin waddled like a duck; maybe you can hop like a kangaroo! How about some props, like a fly swatter or a stuffed toy—anything you think might work with your routine to make it funnier. Stand in front of a mirror, especially if you're dressing up or doing impersonations. You'll need to see if your characters are working for you. Whatever you come up with, have a blast!

5. Before you actually start telling jokes, have a strategy for opening and closing your routine. First, introduce yourself in some humorous way like, "Hi there, I'm Jason the Joke-Teller (or Caitlin the Comedian), and I'm here to make you laugh" (take a short pause . . . then say) "I hope!" This is just one way, but it's funny and it will help to loosen up the audience. Don't forget observational humor based on whatever's happening at that very moment. Make a comment about the weather or a current event or something unusual that's going on in the room—something your audience can relate to, such as "I can see that many of you are smiling, which means your mouth is at least halfway to laughing at my jokes!" Your intro will help to warm up both you and your audience. This is you, improvising as you go along. Then launch into a couple of your funniest jokes, sprinkle a few others through the middle section, and save the rest of the funniest ones for last.

As you move along with your show, telling your jokes, remember that you always have the option to improvise and add funny comments that occur to you at that moment. At the end, during the applause, thank everyone for coming and laughing and tell them what a great audience they were. Take a bow and you're out of there. Now, that was fun, right?

6. Does "practice" sound boring—no fun at all? Think of it this way—you don't get up in front of a bunch of people to play a musical instrument like a guitar or a saxophone without lots of practice, right? Same thing with telling jokes. The more you practice and rehearse your act, the better (and funnier) your jokes will be.

7. Stage fright is no fun (even famous comedians get it sometimes), but there are simple ways to overcome it. First of all, know all your jokes inside and out. As I said before, this takes lots of practice. You want to feel comfortable with your jokes so you don't tell them wrong.

Just before starting your routine, take slow, deep breaths to relax yourself. Make eye contact with a couple of people right away (it helps you forget that there's a big audience watching), and then pretend that everyone else is in their underwear! Pretty crazy advice, but many performers swear that it works. Have complete confidence in yourself; believe in your own funniness. Many famous public speakers start off with a joke to help them overcome stage fright. You're lucky, because you get to tell a whole bunch of jokes. Remember, this is for fun, and once you get people laughing, any stage fright will just melt away.

8. Screwing up a joke, especially in front of an audience, sounds scary, right? But you can recover quickly just by making a joke—out of messing up a joke. If you do mess up a punch line, you could say something like, "Gee, that joke went perfectly when I practiced it in front of the mirror at home! Next time I'll bring the mirror." Almost everything can be funny, so making a joke out of a bad situation can change it into something that you and your audience can laugh at.

9. Keeping your audience's attention boils down to how many laughs you're getting out of them. If they're not laughing, make a joke out of it, and keep your show moving. Focus, and pay attention to what you're doing and how your audience is reacting. Mention names or places your audience will know—this makes their ears perk up. Speak clearly and loudly enough—be sure not to mumble or they won't hear the jokes. Timing is important—take cues from your audience. Pausing for a second or so after your setup will prepare the audience for the punch line and, ultimately, the roar of laughter. It's O.K. to laugh at your own jokes, but make sure your audience laughs first. Don't try too hard. Lighten up—it's only a joke!

10. Some jokes should be avoided. Long ones are tough, because it's hard to keep the audience's attention. Short jokes are best because you get to the punch line (and the laughs) a lot quicker. Offensive jokes (mean-spirited toward people, places, things, etc.) and "dirty" jokes (you know what I'm talking about) have got to be off-limits. Remember, your routine is rated "G" for general audiences.

11. Perform your routine for friends at a birthday party or a sleepover, or maybe during the holidays when you have a lot of family and friends around. Be a part of a talent show your school puts on. Get up onstage with tons of great material stuffed in your brain and tell a whole bunch of very funny jokes. You'll have lots of fun, and so will your audience! That's the reason you're doing this, right? It feels good to make people laugh, and to know that you have entertained them is extremely cool!

11½.

What has four wheels and flies?

Answer: A garbage truck.
(As told by Groucho Marx.)

Doctor! Doctor! I keep thinking I'm a comedian.

You must be joking!